Snap books® Crafts

Updos

Cool Hairstyles for All Occasions

by Jen Jones

Capstone press®

Mankato, Minnesota

Snap Books are published by Capstone Press,
151 Good Counsel Drive, P.O. Box 669, Mankato, Minnesota 56002.
www.capstonepress.com

Library of Congress Cataloging-in-Publication Data
Jones, Jen.
  Updos: cool hairstyles for all occasions / by Jen Jones.
  p. cm. — (Snap books. Crafts)
  Includes bibliographical references and index.
  Summary: "A do-it-yourself crafts book for children and pre-teens on updos and other
hairstyles" — Provided by publisher.
  ISBN-13: 978-1-4296-2313-1 (hardcover)
  ISBN-10: 1-4296-2313-6 (hardcover)
  1. Ornamental hairwork — Juvenile literature. 2. Hairstyles — Juvenile literature. I. Title. II. Series.
TT976.J65 2009
646.7'24 — dc22   2008026952

Editor: Kathryn Clay
Designer: Juliette Peters
Photo Researcher: Marcie Spence
Photo Shoot Stylist: Sarah L. Schuette
Photo Shoot Scheduler: Marcy Morin

Photo Credits:
All photography by Capstone Press/Karon Dubke except:
Bridgeman Art Library International/Yale Center for British Art, Paul Mellon Collection, USA/Miss Sarah
Campbell, 1777-78 (oil on canvas), Reynolds, Sir Joshua (1723-92), 28; Capstone Press/TJ Thoraldson Digital
Photography, 7 (all), 13 (bottom right), 25 (bottom left); Getty Images Inc./American Idol/Frank Micelotta, 29;
Getty Images Inc./The Bridgeman Art Library, 30; Photodisc, 3, 12, 13, 16, 22, 24 (flowers)

1 2 3 4 5 6 14 13 12 11 10 09

The Capstone Press Photo Studio thanks Shylah Cassidy and Dalaina Sandland for their hair styling skills.

Table of Contents

CHAPTER 1

Swept Away

Stargaze at any red carpet. What do female movie stars and pop singers all have in common? Sure they're all wearing glamorous gowns, but they also have amazing updos. These leading ladies know that updos give you instant star quality. Updos are a fast, fun way to transform your look. In just minutes, you can go from grungy to glamorous or punk rock to princess. Talk about makeover magic!

The styles in this book are a snap to do on your own or with a friend. But some updos require the help of a seasoned stylist. If you've got your eye on a more sophisticated style, step into a salon for a quick consultation. Together, you can experiment to find the best updo for you. Pack your picks and fire up your curling irons. It's time to create beautiful updos!

Through Thick and Thin

When it comes to styling, hair types are as different as snowflakes. Whether your hair is curly, wavy, or straight, knowing how to work with your hair type is a must. Find out your secret style weapon.

Thick vs. Thin

For thin hair, maintaining an updo can be quite a challenge. To add texture, apply volumizing spray to the roots. Volumizing shampoos and other products are also available to pack extra punch. You'll also need lots of bobby pins on hand. For those with thick tresses, an extra-hold styling gel will help keep you looking lovely. Half-updos are also a great option for taming wild manes.

Curly vs. Straight

Are you rockin' ringlets or showing off stick-straight locks? Either way, there are plenty of updos just for you. And if your desired updo calls for altering your natural look, never fear. Curly girls can use a flatiron and straightening balm to smooth things out. Straight-haired types can achieve waves with rollers, curling irons, and holding spray.

CHAPTER 2

Before You Begin

Style Secrets

Want to make sure your updo doesn't turn into an up-don't? Here are the secrets to lovely locks.

Skimp on the shampoo.

Believe it or not, it's best not to wash your hair the day of updo styling. Freshly washed hair doesn't hold a style as well as unwashed hair.

Be shirt smart.

Nothing is worse than seeing an updo come tumbling down. Wear a button-down shirt during styling. Pulling a T-shirt over your head after styling could bring on major tress distress.

Take your style for a test run.

Play it safe by practicing the style before the big day.

Tress Toolbox

Just like a chef needs the right ingredients, a smart stylist always keeps the right products on hand. Below are some materials you might want to have handy:

- hairbrush
- wide-toothed comb
- hair clips
- hair rollers
- flatiron and/or curling iron
- bobby pins
- coated elastic ponytail holders
- hairspray
- shine serum

Bring on the Bling

Create sparkle and shine by adding decorative items to your updo. Jeweled bobby pins, rhinestone clips, flowers, and ribbons are sure to enhance any look. If you want to be a daring diva, a tiara can add the ultimate elegance.

CHAPTER 3

Easy Does It: Everyday Updos

Meet Me Halfway

Longing for a softer, more classic look? Leave half of your hair down to beautifully frame that fabulous face of yours.

Half Updo

1 Use a curling iron or hot rollers to create long, loose waves all over your head.

2 Gather hair from the sides and the top. Pull hair into a half-ponytail. Secure hair with a clip or a barrette rather than a ponytail holder.

3 Fan out the hair by loosening pieces from the clip. If you'd like, you can even pull a few pieces loose to create ringlets in front.

finished hairstyle

Let Loose

Ever wish you could roll out of bed and instantly look amazing? With this messy style, you'll look like you did. This loose ponytail goes perfectly with everything from blue jeans to ball gowns.

Star secrets: Both Vanessa Hudgens and Ashley Tisdale of High School Musical have been spotted around Hollywood sporting this look.

Loose Ponytail

1 Use a brush to pull your hair into a high ponytail. Secure hair with a ponytail holder. Leave out some hair on the sides.

2 Backcomb your bangs to add height.

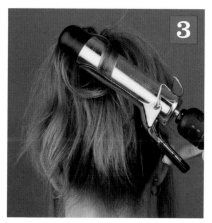

3 Use a curling iron to create soft curls within the ponytail. Then curl the hair that's on the sides of the ponytail.

4 finished hairstyle

Helpful hint: To backcomb your hair, comb small sections of hair in the opposite direction that it grows. This adds lots of volume to flat hair.

CHAPTER 4

Hair with Flair

Twist and Shout

Want an elegant way to keep your hair out of your face? The French twist is a simple solution. This updo will have you shouting "C'est magnifique."

French Twist

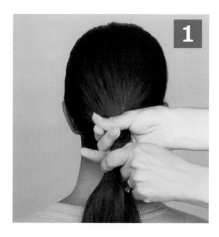

1 Gather all of your hair in a low ponytail near the top of your neck. Hold the hair in your hand rather than securing with a ponytail holder.

2 Twist and lift the hair upward. Continue twisting until you've reached the end of the hair.

3 Hold the twist in place near the top of your head. Tuck the excess top hair underneath the existing twist. Use bobby pins to hold the twist in place.

4

finished hairstyle

Switch it up: It's easy to put a fun spin on the French twist. Instead of tucking the top part under, gather the hair in a claw clip at the top. Let the extra hair spill out in a casual ponytail.

Classy Chignon

A chignon (SHEEN-yon) is a fancy word for a sleek bun. It might be hard to pronounce, but it's super easy to create.

Side Chignon

1 Pull hair into a low side ponytail, securing it with a ponytail holder.

2 Take the top third of the ponytail and create an upward loop by wrapping it around two fingers. Use a bobby pin to hold down the hair just above the ponytail holder.

3 Separate the remaining hair into two sections. Repeat step 2 with the left section. The loop should go off to the left side. Use bobby pins to hold the hair in place.

4 Repeat step 3 on the right side. The loop should go off to the right side.

finished hairstyle

The 'Tweener

Calling all mid-length beauties. Take your shoulder-length hair to the next level with this trendy updo. After all, a chic style doesn't always require extra-long hair.

Shoulder-Length Updo

1 Separate your hair into four sections: front, back, left side, and right side. The front section should be 3 inches (8 centimeters) wide.

2 Remove the clips on the sides. Gather the left and right sides on the top of your head. Secure with a hair clip.

3 Take the front section and use it to cover the clipped section. Use bobby pins to secure hair in place at the back of your head.

4 Take the back section upward to meet the other sections and bobby pin it in place.

5 Use a curling iron to curl the hair that sticks out.

finished hairstyle

Helpful hint: Pull out a few loose tendrils in front and curl with a curling iron.

CHAPTER 5

Special Occasion Styles

Crisscross Cutie

A zigzag part is the perfect way to show off your style. All your friends will beg you to teach them this cute and contemporary look.

Zigzag Pigtails

Helpful hint: If you're having trouble creating the zigzag part, never fear. Special products are available to help you out. Check out an inexpensive tool like the Part Pizazz or Styl Styk.

 **1** Use a flatiron to straighten your hair.

 **2** Starting near your forehead, use a comb to slide your part from side to side. This will create a zigzag pattern.

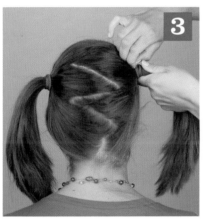 **3** Continue the zigzag pattern through your hair to the top of your neck. Separate your hair into two ponytails, and secure with ponytail holders.

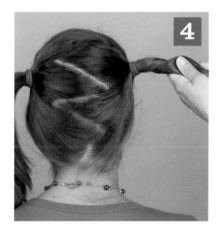 **4** On one side, twist from top to ¾ of the way down.

 **5** Wrap the twisty part into a bun. Use bobby pins to secure the bun on your head.

 **6** Repeat steps 4 and 5 on the other side. Use hair gel to spike the hair that sticks out of the buns.

finished hairstyle

Who Likes Spikes?

If you want all eyes on you, check out this unforgettable updo. Caution: this look is meant for daring divas only.

Helpful hint: To add even more flair to this look, add hair extensions in fun colors like green or purple.

Spiky Style

 **1** Use a flatiron to straighten your hair.

 **2** Divide your hair into six or more sections. The number of sections you create will depend on how many spots you want to stick out.

 **3** Gather a section of hair. Twist it from the top to ¾ of the way down.

 **4** Wrap the twisty part into a small bun. Use bobby pins to secure the bun to your head. Use ultra-strong hairspray to spike the remaining hair.

 **5** Repeat steps 3 and 4 for each section of hair.

 **6**

finished hairstyle

Going Glam

Want to go all out with your look? This is the updo for you. Though this style takes a little more work, it's perfect for a special occasion.

Fit for a Queen

Apply a small amount of shine serum to your hair.

Gather your hair in a high ponytail, securing it with a ponytail holder. Separate a 2-inch (5-centimeter) section of hair in front.

Take out small sections of hair and curl them with a curling iron to create large loops.

Use bobby pins to secure the loops to your head.

Repeat steps 3 and 4 until all the hair is out of the ponytail and looped on your head.

Sweep the front hair across your forehead. Pin in place with a bobby pin. Add a tiara or glittery headband to top off the look.

finished hairstyle

23

CHAPTER 6

When Less is More

Yes, it's true: most updo styles are geared for medium-length hair or longer. Yet short-haired girls don't have to get the short end of the style stick! Why pay big bucks for extensions when there are plenty of ways for short hair to go glam?

Twist Top

Grab a handful of jeweled clips for this fun look. Starting by your right ear, take a 1-inch (2.5-centimeter) section of hair and twist it. Attach a clip behind the twisted part to hold it in place. Continue doing so across your head until you have a "headband" of clips.

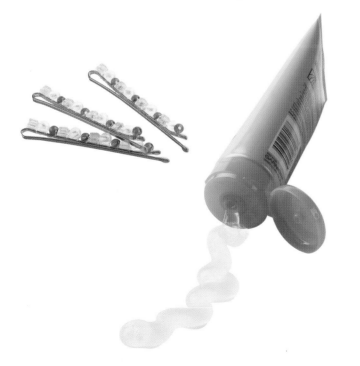

Short Hair Help

Shape is the key for short hair. Use styling gel for a slicker effect, and backcomb your hair for maximum height. Add sparkly clips or jeweled bobby pins for even more shine.

CHAPTER 7

Quick Fixes

You don't always have all day to fix your hair. Sometimes you need a great look in a hurry. If leaving your locks down just won't do, try one of these ultra-quick updo ideas. You'll be the only one who knows how easy it was to create.

Total Tease (right)

Separate a broad section of your hair in front. Holding the section straight up, use a brush to backcomb hair and add height. After creating your perfect poof, secure the hair with a barrette or ponytail holder. Even though this style is only a half-updo, it's 100 percent fabulous!

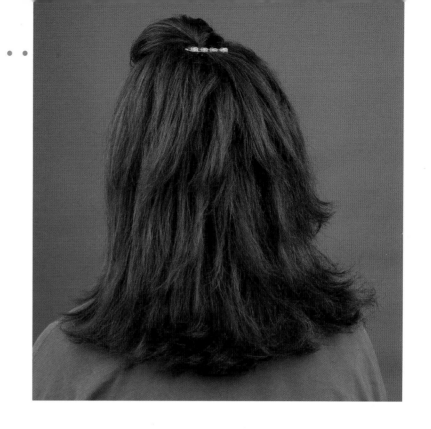

Picture Perfect Pony (left)

Gather and secure your hair in a sleek high ponytail. Take a 1-inch (2.5-centimeter) section of hair and wrap it around, pinning the end in place. (The hair wraparound should hide the ponytail holder.) Tease the top part of the ponytail to add height and volume. Optional: Use a large-barrel curling iron to add a fun flip at the bottom.

CHAPTER 8

Up-Don'ts

Updo doesn't mean "overdo." For certain styles, simplicity rules. Check out these updos gone wrong for examples of what not to do!

Old-School Updos

In the 18th century, ladies sported truly larger-than-life locks. Big, tall beehives were fashionable — and the higher, the better. Some women even stored mini-birdcages (complete with birds) inside their wacky weaves!

Even celebrities have bad hair days. Just ask American Idol's Sanjaya Malakar or pop singer Jessica Simpson. In 2007, Sanjaya's hair hit a sour note with his now famous faux-hawk.

Jessica didn't fare much better when she wore a mile-high beehive to a red-carpet event. This look earned her not-so-flattering comparisons to Marge Simpson.

Though these styles are definitely up-don'ts, feel free to let your own creativity shine when designing new styles. Anything that shows off your unique personality and beauty is sure to make a fierce fashion statement.

Sanjaya Malakar

Fun Facts

- A major annual touring event, "Hair Wars" brings together top stylists in the United States to go head-to-head — literally. Live models sport creative updos that have featured live snakes, helicopter propellers, and spider webs. It's quite a beauty battle.

- Did you know the average human scalp has more than 100,000 hairs? It's no wonder there are hundreds of updos to choose from.

- The owner of the ultimate updo might just be France's Marie Antoinette. This legendary queen's hair was all the rage in the 1700s.  She sported an updo that was 3-feet (1-meter) high. It was decorated with everything from food to toy boats.

Glossary

chic (SHEEK) — a fashionable style

chignon (SHEEN-yon) — a smooth bun gathered near the neck

consultation (kan-sel-TAY-shun) — a meeting to discuss an idea or an outcome

extensions (ik-STEN-shuns) — fake or real hair that is attached to your own hair to add length or volume

ringlet (RING-lit) — a curled piece of hair

serum (SIHR-um) — a product that makes hair shiny

tendril (TEN-drel) — a piece of hair that is long, slender, and curly

volumizing (vol-yem-MIES-ing) — adding texture and volume

Read More

Jones, Jen. *Braiding Hair: Beyond the Basics*. Crafts. Mankato, Minn.: Capstone Press, 2009.

Neuman, Maria. *Fabulous Hair*. New York: Dorling Kindersley, 2006.

Warrick, Leanne. *Hair Trix for Cool Chix: The Real Girl's Guide to Great Hair*. Cool Chix. New York: Watson-Guptill, 2004.

Internet Sites

FactHound offers a safe, fun way to find educator-approved Internet sites related to this book.

Here's what you do:

1. Visit *www.facthound.com*
2. Choose your grade level.
3. Begin your search.

This book's ID number is 9781429623131.

FactHound will fetch the best sites for you!

About the Author

Curly girl Jen Jones has been obsessed with hairstyles ever since she was a little girl. Although Jen didn't grow up to be a hairstylist, she is now a Los Angeles-based writer who has authored more than 30 books for Capstone Press.

Her stories have been published in magazines such as *American Cheerleader*, *Dance Spirit*, *Ohio Today*, and *Pilates Style*.

She has also written for E! Online and PBS Kids, as well as being a Web site producer for major talk shows such as *The Jenny Jones Show*, *The Sharon Osbourne Show*, and *The Larry Elder Show*.

Index